Fresh vegetables from the farms on the banks of the Nile River.

A travelling salesman passes from village to village.

An open-air butcher shop.

EGYPT
the land

Arlene Moscovitch

A Bobbie Kalman Book

The Lands, Peoples, and Cultures Series

Crabtree Publishing Company

The Lands, Peoples, and Cultures Series

Created by Bobbie Kalman

Coordinating editor
Ellen Rodger

Project development
First Folio Resource Group, Inc.
Pauline Beggs
Tom Dart
Kathryn Lane
Debbie Smith

Editing
Joyce Funamoto

Photo research
Robyn Craig

Design
David Vereschagin/Quadrat Communications

Separations and film
Dot 'n Line Image Inc.

Printer
Worzalla Publishing Company

Special thanks to
Sally Abuseif, Heather Dalgleish, Prof. Dr.
Ahmed ElSherbini, Consul, Bureau of
Cultural and Education Affairs of Egypt;
Dr. N. B. Millet, Senior Curator, Egyptian
Section, Royal Ontario Museum; André L.
Potvin, Ms. Elham Yassin

Photographs
AP/Wide World Photos: p. 16; Marcello Bertinetti/Photo
Researchers: p. 8 (bottom); Corbis/Digital image © 1996
Corbis – original image courtesy of NASA: p. 10 (right);
Corbis/Kevin Schafer: p. 28 (left); Corbis/Lawson Wood:
p. 29 (bottom); Marc Crabtree: cover, title page, front
endpaper page 1 (top, middle,), page 2 (top), rear endpaper
page 2 (top, middle), pp. 4–5, p. 7 (right), p. 10 (left), p. 12
(all), p. 14, p. 15 (top), p. 18 (left), p. 19 (top), p. 24 (both),
p. 26 (right), p. 27 (top), p. 29 (top left), pp. 30–31 (all); Peter
Crabtree: front endpaper page 1 (bottom), page 2 (middle,
bottom), rear endpaper page 1 (all), page 2 (bottom two), p. 17
(bottom), p. 19 (bottom), p. 20, p. 23 (bottom), p. 27 (bottom);
Stephen Dalton/Photo Researchers: p. 29 (top right); Georg
Gerster/Photo Researchers: p. 7 (left), p. 17 (top), p. 21, p. 26
(left); Imapress/Archive Photos: p. 13 (top); Franke
Keating/Photo Researchers: p. 11; Guy W. Midkiff: p. 8 (top),
p. 15 (bottom), p. 23 (top); John Mitchell/Photo Researchers:
p. 28 (right); Carl Purcell: p. 9 (bottom), p. 13 (bottom), p. 18
(right), p. 25 (top); Reuters/Str/Archive Photos: p. 25
(bottom); SEF/Art Resource, NY: p. 3; H. T. Wright: p. 9 (top)

Every effort has been made to obtain the appropriate credit and
full copyright clearance for all images in this book. Any oversites,
despite Crabtree's greatest precautions, will be corrected in
future editions.

Map
Jim Chernishenko

Illustrations
William Kimber. The pyramids of Giza appear at the head of
each section. The Great Sphinx is shown on the back cover.

Cover: The ancient Step Pyramid rises above lush farm land.

Title page: A farmer works in his fields.

Published by
Crabtree Publishing Company

PMB 16A, 350 Fifth Ave.	360 York Road, RR 4,	73 Lime Walk
Suite 3308	Niagara-on-the-Lake,	Headington
New York	Ontario, Canada	Oxford OX3 7AD
N.Y. 10118	L0S 1J0	United Kingdom

Cataloging in Publication Data
Moscovitch, Arlene, 1946-
    Egypt, the land / Arlene Moscovitch
        p. cm. -- (The lands, peoples, and cultures series)
    Includes index.
        Summary: Introduces the geography, weather, cities, ancient
monuments, wildlife, and more in the land of Egypt.
        4-9.
        ISBN 0-86505-232-8 (RLB). -- ISBN 0-86505-312-X (paper)
    1. Egypt--Description and travel Juvenile literature.
    [1. Egypt.] I. Title. II. Title: Egypt. III.Series.
DT56.2.M67 200⌐
962--dc21
                                                LC 99-16591
                                                CIP

Contents

Egypt: The ageless land

In the sun-scorched land of Egypt, the ancient and modern worlds live side by side. For more than 5000 years, Egypt has been home to many different cultures. The kings, or **Pharaohs**, of ancient Egypt ruled over this great **civilization** for 30 centuries. They were followed by **conquerors** from the lands of ancient Greece and Rome.

We know a lot about Egypt's long history. Some of its history is written on **papyrus**, a type of paper made from a plant that grows in Egypt's **fertile** Nile River Valley. Some of its history is written in ancient stone **temples**, on statues, and in **tombs**, such as the famous **pyramids**.

There is much more to Egypt than its ancient history. It is a bustling land with sprawling cities, massive dams, busy farmers' fields, and noisy factories. Flocks of birds gather along the Nile River and catfish swim in its muddy riverbed. Beyond the waters of the Nile, deserts seem to stretch forever.

Facts at a glance

Official name: Arab Republic of Egypt
(Jumhuriyat Misr al-Arabiyah)

Capital city: Cairo (al-Qahira)

Population: 60 million

Area: 1,001,449 square kilometers
(386,660 square miles)

Official language: Arabic

Main religion: Islam

Currency: One Egyptian pound = 100 piasters

National holiday: July 23, Revolution Day

⛰ Land of contrasts ⛰

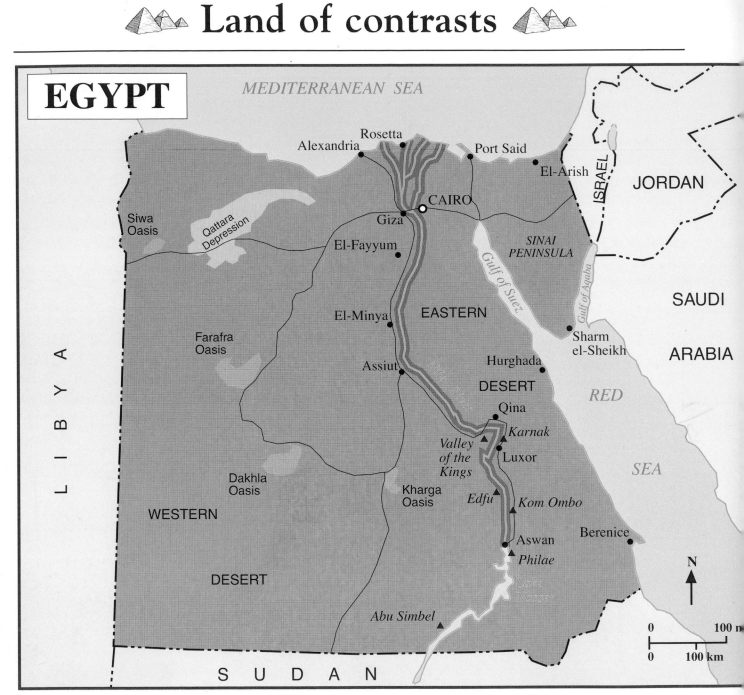

EGYPT

MEDITERRANEAN SEA

Alexandria • Rosetta • Port Said • El-Arish

JORDAN
ISRAEL

CAIRO ○
Giza

Siwa Oasis

Qattara Depression

El-Fayyum

SINAI PENINSULA

Gulf of Suez

Gulf of Aqaba

SAUDI

El-Minya

EASTERN

Sharm el-Sheikh

ARABIA

L I B Y A

Farafra Oasis

Assiut

Hurghada

Nile River

DESERT

RED

Qina

Dakhla Oasis

Kharga Oasis

Karnak ▲
Valley of the Kings ▲ Luxor

SEA

WESTERN

Edfu ▲ Kom Ombo ▲

Berenice

DESERT

Aswan ▲ Philae

N

Lake Nasser

Abu Simbel ▲

0   100 n
0   100 km

S U D A N

Red triangles on map represent temples.

Egypt is a country of striking contrasts. In this square-shaped country, there are deserts where almost nothing grows, but there is also some of the richest farmland in the world. Tall mountains reach into the sky, while salty depressions plunge far below sea level. Egypt is divided into four different land regions: the Nile River Valley and Delta, the Western Desert, the Eastern Desert, and the Sinai Peninsula.

The Nile River Valley

The Nile River Valley is a green ribbon of fertile land that lies on either side of the great Nile River. The valley contains some of the richest soil in the world, which the Egyptians call *kemet*, or "black land." Here, farmers plant fields of cotton, sugar cane, and date palms. The Nile River Valley, which takes up only 7 percent of the country, is also where 85 percent of Egypt's population lives.

The Western Desert

The Western Desert has two other names. It is sometimes called the Libyan Desert and sometimes called "The Sea of Sand." This desert has shifting **sand dunes**, or huge mounds of sand, large clumps of rock, and **oases.** An oasis is a pleasant green spot in the middle of the desert, where plants and water appear. Oases are fed by underground **springs.** These springs make life possible for plants, animals, and people.

Sand dunes on the march

The desert is spreading. Sand dunes move about three kilometers (almost two miles) every five years. The wind constantly blows grains of sand in one direction until they form huge dunes. The dunes cover everything in their path, even palm trees and houses.

Barren sand dunes roll beyond the fertile shore of the Nile River.

Houses on the edge of the town of el Gedida are swallowed by the Western Desert.

7

Once, people rode camels across the Western Desert. Now, it is much more common to travel by truck.

The Eastern Desert

The Eastern, or Arabian, Desert lies between the Nile River and the Red Sea. This area is rich in oil, minerals, and stone. Red rocky hills and high mountains rise to over 2000 meters (6560 feet) on the eastern coast.

The Sinai Peninsula

The Sinai Peninsula is a land bridge between Africa and Asia. Even though it is almost totally surrounded by water, this area is mainly desert. Throughout the Sinai Desert are long narrow valleys called **wadis.** Over thousands of years, the wadis were carved out by heavy rains that fell on the mountains.

The monks of Saint Catherine's Monastery live in the Sinai Desert at the base of Mount Sinai, the tallest mountain in Egypt.

Rugged hills rise from the flat sands of the Eastern Desert.

A diver explores the coral reefs of the Red Sea, off the southern coast of the Sinai Peninsula.

The Nile: River of life

To the ancient Egyptians, the Nile River was not only a river, but also a god. In a country where rain almost never falls and 93 percent of the land is desert, its waters are often the only source of life for people, animals, and plants.

The Nile Delta

The Nile is the longest river in the world. It stretches for an amazing 6670 kilometers (4150 miles). The triangle-shaped area of land where the river meets the Mediterranean Sea is called the Nile Delta. The word "delta" is the Greek word for the letter D. The shape of the letter delta, Δ, is the same shape as the river's mouth. The Mediterranean Sea is slowly washing away parts of the Nile Delta, so there is less land for farming than there used to be.

From the sky, the green of the Nile Valley stands out against the surrounding desert. Cairo, the largest city in Africa, is the mass of gray.

The Nile and its seasons

The ancient Egyptians depended on the Nile to survive, so they studied the river's changes very carefully. They eventually noticed a pattern. The river had three seasons. *Akhet* was the season of the flood, from July to October. During this time, farmers could not grow crops, so they repaired their tools and prepared for the growing season. *Peret*, from November to February, was the season when the waters fell. It was the time to plow the fields, sow the crops, and build new **irrigation** channels. *Shemu*, from March to June, was the harvest season. During this time, people had to work very hard, harvesting all the crops before *Akhet*, when the waters rose again.

*Egyptian sailboats, called **fellucas**, glide between the islands of the Nile.*

The Aswan High Dam

The Aswan High Dam was one of the world's largest construction sites. In the 1960s, 30,000 people toiled for almost ten years to complete the project. The dam was built to control the water level of the Nile and to prevent huge floods. After the dam was built, the flow of water from the Nile was controlled so that farmers could grow their crops all year long.

Water blasts from the Aswan High Dam and roars down the Nile. The power of the water is used to create electricity for Egypt.

The dam has helped Egypt, but it has caused some problems too. When the dam was built, a huge lake called Lake Nasser was created behind it. This lake flooded many villages and buried precious, ancient temples.

11

The majority of today's Egyptians are a mix of all the peoples who settled around the Nile Delta, in the north, over thousands of years. Most Egyptians speak Arabic, the language of the Arabs who came to Egypt from the Middle East about 1400 years ago. People also settled further south along the Nile River and in the desert, where they adapted to the sometimes harsh conditions of the land on which they lived.

Nubians

Nubians have lived in the south of Egypt and in the neighboring country of Sudan for thousands of years. They have their own language, traditions, and customs. When the Aswan High Dam was built, the Nubians' way of life was threatened. Lake Nasser flooded their fields and villages. Some Nubians headed north to find new jobs and homes in the cities. Others moved to new Nubian villages built in areas that were safe from flooding.

A Nubian farmer surveys his fields on the banks of Lake Nasser.

(above) Many Egyptian women cover their heads with a scarf. It not only shades them from the sun, but is also is a sign of modesty in Egyptian culture.

(right) Children walk to school together in Cairo.

12

The people of the Siwa Oasis gather outside of town for a festival.

Bedouin rest during a long journey through the Sinai Desert.

The people of the Western Desert

The desert is a harsh place to live, so few people choose to make it their home. Some people, like the Siwans, have settled on oases where water is readily available. At the oases, tall green palm trees stand out from the brown desert sand. Narrow alleyways lead to shady walled gardens. Life moves at a slower pace on an oasis. With new roads and more contact with the rest of Egypt, the lives of the villagers are slowly changing pace.

The Bedouin

Traditionally, the Bedouin are a **nomadic** people. They travel the desert with their herds of goats and camels. They settle in one place for a few weeks or months. Then, the Bedouin pack up their belongings and move on, searching the desert for another suitable site to set up camp. They live in cozy tents with low ceilings. Colorful rugs and pillows cover the sandy desert floor. The Bedouin way of life is changing, too. More and more, the Bedouin are moving to permanent shelters.

Even though more than half of Egypt is covered by desert, **agriculture** is an important industry, thanks to the Nile River. For over 5000 years, Egyptian farmers, who are known as *fellahin*, have thought of different ways to move water from the Nile River to their fields. They usually grow enough food to feed themselves, and then one other crop to sell for cash.

Irrigating the land

All along the Nile River, an irrigation system of canals and drains carries water to and from villages and farms. Many canals were built thousands of years ago. To take water from the canals to their fields, some farmers use modern pumps. Others follow the older, more traditional ways. The *sakia* is a kind of waterwheel that was invented many centuries ago. A water buffalo walks around in a circle, pulling a pole that turns the *sakia*. Then, the *sakia*'s buckets scoop up water from the canal.

A farmer gives his child a ride on the lever of a sakia.

Archimedes screw

For more than 2000 years, *fellahin* have been using the ancient Greek Archimedes Screw to water their fields. Farmers put one end of a small pump in the canal. They sit by the side of the canal and crank the pump's handle. Water is forced out of the canal, up the pump, and onto the farmers' fields.

14

(above) Perched on the edge of a fishing boat, a man pulls in his nets from the Nile.

(right) High up in the branches of a palm tree, a picker drops dates into a basket.

Crops

At the edge of the desert, *fellahin* grow crops such as cotton, wheat, rice, corn, onions, and potatoes. Many farmers also grow date palm trees. Every part of the tree is used. People eat the sticky, sweet dates. They build carts, houses, and stables from the thick trunks. Palm leaves are woven into mats and baskets. Even the palm stems are split at the ends to make brooms.

Fishing families

Some families fish from large rowing boats in the Nile River. Usually, adults row the boats while children throw out nets to catch the fish. They catch Nile perch, which can grow as large as 136 kilograms (300 pounds), and tiger fish, which have razor-sharp teeth!

In Egypt, there is a lot of sun and very little rain throughout the year. Most of the time, the climate is hot and dry. Egypt has only two seasons: the cool winter from November to April and the very hot summer from May to October. The temperatures become higher the further south you go. On the Mediterranean coast, where it rains the most, it can reach 31°C (88°F) in the summer. At Aswan, in the south, the thermometer sometimes reads a scorching 50°C (122°F)!

Chilly desert nights

Most people think of the desert as a very hot place, but the desert is usually cold at night. There are no trees or grass to trap the heat, so the air becomes very chilly when the sun goes down. During the winter months, the temperature can drop to the freezing point.

On a sweltering day in Cairo, a couple cannot resist the cool waters of the Nile – even with their clothes on!

A burning wind

The *khamsin* is a hot, dry desert wind that blows from the south each spring. The *khamsin* can whip clouds of flying sand up to 150 kilometers (93 miles) an hour. When the *khamsin* blows, sand covers everything and gets in people's and animals' eyes. During a *khamsin*, the temperature can rise 20°C (about 68°F) in just a few hours. The dust can swirl so fiercely that it can sweep up small creatures, bury roads, and even block the view of pilots flying in the area. *Khamsin* is the Arabic word for 50. People gave this name to the burning wind because it can last for 50 days. Fortunately, this rarely happens!

Rain and drought

Egypt's water comes mainly from the Nile River and not from the sky as rain. The city of Alexandria on the Mediterranean coast receives the most rain, about nineteen centimeters (seven inches) every winter. As you go further away from the Mediterranean coast, the amount of rain decreases sharply. **Droughts**, or long periods of dry weather, happen in the south of Egypt almost every summer. Now that Egypt has the Aswan High Dam, water can be stored in a **reservoir** and used during times of drought.

Plants push up through the dry earth after a rare flood in the Western Desert.

A merchant sells his wares from a bridge. It crosses one of the many canals that brings water inland from the Nile.

Transportation, then and now

Egyptians mix old and new ways of getting around when they travel in the desert, on the water, and through cities and villages.

Waterways

Egypt's first highway was the Nile River. Thousands of years ago, people and goods traveled along the river in boats and rafts made of papyrus stems tied together. They added oars and a sail to catch the wind. Egyptian sailboats, called *feluccas*, still carry passengers and goods up and down the Nile. They share the river with motorboats and cruise ships. The newer boats may be faster and bigger, but the *feluccas* are much more graceful.

Anchored ships wait to pay a toll before entering the Suez Canal. The average toll is $70,000 U.S.

The Suez Canal

Thousands of years ago, the Egyptians tried to dig a channel to connect the Red Sea, which lies to the east of Egypt, and the Mediterranean Sea to the north. Since then, many people have wanted to build a canal to join the two seas. They knew this route would shorten the distance for trading ships moving between Europe and Asia.

The seas were finally joined when the Suez Canal was opened in 1869. Thousands of people worked for eleven years to build it. When it was finished, the Egyptian ruler, Ismail Pasha, threw a huge party that lasted for days. His celebration cost so much money that he ended up having to sell Egypt's share of the canal to England in 1875. It was 1956 before the Egyptians controlled the canal again.

*Sails on **feluccas** are made of long strips of cloth sewn together. Their huge size means that they can catch a lot of wind.*

Traveling through the Suez Canal

Today, as many as 40 ships travel through the Suez Canal each day. The canal is 193 kilometers (120 miles) long and the trip takes between ten and twelve hours. The canal is too narrow for two-way traffic, so a convoy of boats leaves the north end at the same time that a convoy leaves the south end. The two convoys pass each other in Bitter Lake, where the canal widens.

Camels

Camels, sometimes called "ships of the desert," are another form of transportation. For thousands of years, they have carried people, their belongings, and merchandise from place to place. Their large padded feet do not slip on the constantly shifting desert sand. They can travel for days without food or water. They live off the fat and fluids stored in their hump. Camels can also close their nostrils to keep sand out and moisture in. These days, camels share the desert with Jeeps, pickup trucks, and cars.

Riding a camel is fun, but a little strange at first. Camels have a bumpy, rolling walk, and they spit when they are unhappy.

City traffic

Cairo, Egypt's capital city, always seems to have a traffic jam. The streets are noisy and crowded with buses, cars, trucks, bicycles, people, and sometimes donkeys. To avoid the traffic, go underground where more than a million people ride the subway in Cairo every day.

Donkey carts are popular in Egypt – even along busy city streets.

The ancient Egyptians were great builders. Thousands of years ago, they constructed temples, pyramids, and other monuments. These **monuments**, scattered throughout Egypt, give us clues about what people believed, where they **worshiped**, and how they lived close to 5000 years ago.

The Great Temple

The Great Temple of Abu Simbel was carved out of a sandstone cliff almost 3500 years ago. The great Pharaoh Ramses II was worshiped as a god and had the temple built to honor himself. Today, four huge statues of Ramses still guard the temple's entrance. Each statue towers more than 20 meters (65 feet) high. A smaller temple stands nearby, dedicated to Ramses' wife, Nefertari. For hundreds of years, Abu Simbel was almost completely covered in sand. Only the heads of Ramses' statues could be seen. The temple was cleared completely of sand in 1919, and all four of the seated statues were finally visible.

The temples that almost drowned

In 1960, these temples faced great danger. Rising waters from the newly built Aswan High Dam were going to flood the area. To rescue the temples, workers cut them into over 1000 numbered blocks. Then, they carefully put the blocks back together exactly as before, but 65 meters (213 feet) above and 210 meters (689 feet) north of their old location. Millions of people all over the world helped pay to save the temples. Although many had never been to Egypt, they did not want the world to lose these treasures.

(opposite) Slowly … carefully … restorers guide Ramses II's face as a crane lifts it to higher ground.

The restorers made sure that the broken head of Ramses II was still at the statue's feet after the Great Temple was moved.

The pyramids of Giza

Egypt's most famous monuments stand on a desert plain at Giza, outside Cairo. The pyramids are gigantic stone monuments that are more than 4500 years old. They were built as tombs for the ancient Pharaohs by thousands of workers. The largest of these, the Great Pyramid of Cheops, weighs 2.3 million tonnes (2.5 million tons). Each stone in the pyramid is as heavy as a small car. The stones of the pyramid were fit together without **mortar**. They are placed so perfectly that a razor blade cannot pass between them. Even today, the Great Pyramid of Cheops is the largest stone structure in the world.

The Great Sphinx

Guarding the pyramids is the famous figure of the Great Sphinx. The Egyptians call this huge statue *Abu'l Hol*, the terrible or awesome one. Its lion's body is 73 meters (240 feet) long and its human head is 20 meters (66 feet) high. Each eye of the Sphinx is about two meters (six feet) tall!

Restoring the Sphinx

For many years, the Sphinx was partly buried in sand, and so it was protected from the destructive wind. Once the Sphinx was uncovered, the soft sandstone did not stand up well to the elements and the Sphinx began to fall apart. People visiting the Sphinx also damaged it. It lost its nose, then its beard. **Restorers** worked very hard to save the Sphinx, but sometimes they did more harm than good! In the 1980s, the Sphinx's left shoulder suddenly collapsed while restorers were working on it. Restoration of this world-famous statue is now complete, but new dangers threaten the Sphinx. The Sphinx is quickly crumbling from air pollution. Water seeping through the ground is also weakening the Sphinx and the pyramids.

The Sphinx, which the Pharaoh Khafre had made out of soft sandstone, is as old as the pyramids. Historians think that the Sphinx's face is Khafre's own face.

Friends visiting the pyramids sit on the huge limestone blocks.

23

Cities

Roads at different levels lessen the amount of traffic in Cairo.

About half of Egypt's population lives in cities. Many people have moved from small villages in search of work. In the cities, most people live in apartments. Some apartments are spacious and some are tiny rooms above shops. Small numbers of people have large houses with gardens.

Cairo

The Arabs who first came to Egypt gave Cairo its name, *"al-Qahira,"* or the Conqueror. Today, Cairo is the largest city in Africa. At least 16 million people live here.

Cairo is divided into districts or quarters. Modern Cairo has new apartments, office buildings, shops, and movie theaters. The old Arab quarter has small shops opening directly on to narrow streets. From the balconies in their apartments, people chat to each other and watch life in the lanes below. In this area, you will find dozens of bustling markets. The Khan el-Khalili market, or *souq*, was founded in the fourteenth century. Even then, this lively market helped make Cairo an important trading center. You can still buy gold, perfume, silk, spices, carpets, glass, and leather in the small shops in the Khan el-Khalili *souq*.

With merchants' displays and shoppers crowding the streets, there is little room for cars in the laneways of Old Cairo.

Alexandria

Alexandria is Egypt's second-largest city. Five million people live in this major port on the Mediterranean Sea. Alexandria stands at the crossroads of Asia in the east and Europe in the west. Its location is one of the reasons that the Greek conqueror Alexander the Great founded the city there in 332 B.C. Centuries ago, the towering lighthouse of Pharos guided ships into the harbor, past Antirhodus Island where palaces and temples stood.

A series of earthquakes followed by a massive tidal wave swept much of the famous city into the harbor 1600 years ago. Recently, after much searching in the waters of Alexandria's harbor, explorers discovered the lost island of Antirhodos. On this submerged island, they found two sphinxes and the remains of the palace of the Egyptian queen, Cleopatra. This famous queen ruled during the first century B.C. Now, historians can find out even more about Cleopatra and this important time in Egypt's history.

Many Egyptians spend their summer vacations in Alexandria, enjoying its white sand beaches and refreshing sea breezes.

Divers steady an ancient sphinx as it is pulled from Alexandria Bay by crane.

Since cotton plants do not grow very tall, children often help pick them during the school holidays.

For over 2000 years, foreign rulers controlled Egypt. Then, in 1952, Egyptians took charge of their own country again. Since then, they have made their old industries stronger and developed new ones. Before, most industries were in Cairo or Alexandria. Now, there are factories and industrial sites throughout the Nile River Valley.

Textiles

Egyptian cotton is among the finest in the world. Egyptians pick cotton from fields along the banks of the Nile River. Trucks take the cotton to the spinning mills, where factory workers spin the cotton fibers into threads. Then, the threads are transported to a weaving mill, where weavers create rolls and rolls of cotton fabric. The fabric is used to make clothes and fine **linens**, which are exported around the world. The cotton sheets you sleep on every night may have been made in Egypt!

Workers load sugar cane onto a freight train. The sugar cane will be made into granulated sugar.

Heavy industry

There are enormous refineries in Egypt that produce steel, iron, and aluminum products. Cement is also a huge industry, since there is so much rock, sand, and gravel in the country. The cement is used to build houses, because there is very little wood in Egypt.

High tech

In Egypt today, more than 200 companies build computers and other electronic items. Some of these products are used in people's homes, some in offices, and some in industry. For instance, Egyptian companies build electronic controls for elevator systems, water heating systems, and washing machines. Many specialists produce computer software or programs for people in Arabic-speaking countries. There is even a company that creates virtual museums!

Tourism

Tourism is one of Egypt's biggest industries. Almost six million people visit the country each year to see the magnificent pyramids, the Sphinx, and other well-known ancient sites. Some Egyptians work as guides, others work in hotels, and still others run souvenir stands. Many sailors take visitors on Nile cruises in their *feluccas*. These days, tourists also come to the Red Sea for their vacation. They snorkel or scuba dive through the plants and brightly colored fishes of the coral reefs.

(left) A student learns on a computer so that one day she may work in Egypt's computer industry.

(below) Tourists visit the Temple of Luxor, Egypt's center of religion in 1550 B.C.

Egypt is home to many different kinds of animals. Most animals live in the desert or by fresh or salt water, but even the cities have a surprising amount of wildlife. It is possible to see a small ferret or mongoose scooting under a car or scampering along one of the narrow alleyways in the old parts of cities and towns.

Desert animals

Many people think that deserts contain nothing but sand, but they are filled with all sorts of creatures, including snakes, sand cats, and small desert foxes called fennecs. These animals have learned to adapt to life in the desert. Since there is little water, they live off the moisture inside the food they eat. They also sleep during the heat of the day and come out at night when it is cool. Certain animals seem to have been made especially for the desert. For example, small wild cats called sand cats have thick mats of fur on the bottom of their paws to protect themselves from the burning sand.

The horned viper escapes the desert heat by burrowing into the sand. Its horns help keep the sand out of its eyes.

Fennecs are the smallest foxes in the world. They are about the size of a small dog.

Dwellers of the Nile

The Nile River Valley provides a home for many species of fish and birds. Hoopoes and turtledoves flit through the date palms and eucalyptus trees. Hawks soar above the water, and cattle egrets wade in the river or perch on top of water buffalo, picking off ticks and other pests. Tilapias, which are also called Egyptian mouth-breeders, swim through the water, **incubating** their babies in their mouths. These fish are careful not to eat at the same time they carry their young, so they do not accidentally swallow them.

Life in the Red Sea

The Red Sea and its shores contain a large variety of wildlife. Rainbow-colored fish dart through the coral reefs along the shores. Further offshore, sharks and dolphins plunge through the waves. One mammal that lives in the Red Sea is the dugong. The dugong is sometimes called the sea cow because it loves to munch on the thick beds of sea grass. The dugong and its relative, the manatee, are the only vegetarian sea mammals.

(above) The scorpion's tail has a poisonous sting.

(left) An egret rests in a farmer's field near the banks of the Nile.

(below) The dugong pushes itself along the sea floor with its flippers when looking for plants to eat. This mammal is now extremely rare in Egypt.

Egypt's rich **civilization** is over 5000 years old. Every day, Egyptians live in the midst of the treasures of their past. They pass by ancient monuments on their way to work. They wander through streets lined with markets and shops built centuries ago. Egyptians are proud of their past, but they are also looking forward to the future. They know that Egypt is part of the modern world, with its own present-day problems to solve.

Population explosion

More than 60 million people live in Egypt. With more than one million babies born every year, the population continues to grow. All these people need food and a place to live. In Egypt, the amount of usable land is shrinking. Only seven percent of the land is good for growing crops. Almost the entire population is crammed into this same tiny area. Cities are so crowded that people have started building high-rise apartments and parking lots on fertile farmland.

A place for everyone

Today, Egyptians are trying to turn parts of their desert into fertile land for farming. They have discovered a huge underground lake stretching for more than 300 kilometers (about 186 miles) below the "Sea of Sand." They are also trying to irrigate parts of the Western Desert. The government hopes that these projects will double the amount of farmland in the country. The government is also working to solve the problem of overcrowding. It is building new cities in the Nile Valley Delta, with homes, office buildings, and factories where people can live and work.

Pollution problems

Cairo is one of the most crowded cities in the world. The daily traffic clogs its streets and pollutes its air. The acid in Cairo's air pollution eats away at ancient treasures, such as the pyramids and the Sphinx. Plants and animals are also affected by pollution. Farmers and factories use chemicals that poison the lakes and the Nile River, harming the wildlife.

Egyptians are trying hard to solve the country's pollution problem.

Protecting Egypt's land and monuments

Egypt is working hard to protect its environment and its rich **heritage** from being destroyed by pollution. The government continues to educate farmers about the effect of **pesticides** and **fertilizers** on crops and on the Nile. Anyone who dumps waste into the Nile River is given a large fine. The government also plans to move roads and houses away from Giza, so that they have less effect on the Great Pyramids.

A restorer carefully injects glue into a cracked carving.

Scaffolding covers an ancient temple's pillars, which restorers are strengthening and repairing.

Glossary

agriculture The practice or science of farming

civilization A society with a well-established culture that has existed for a long period of time

conqueror A person who gains control over a land by using force

drought A long period of time when no rain falls

fertile Able to produce abundant crops or vegetation

fertilizer A material added to soil to make it produce more crops

heritage Customs, objects, and achievements handed down from earlier generations

incubate To provide warmth and other conditions that help eggs develop

irrigation The process of supplying water to land

linens Articles made of cloth such as sheets, tablecloths, and shirts

monument A structure built to remember a person or event

mortar A building material of sand, lime, water, and sometimes cement that holds together bricks or stones

nomadic Having no fixed home and moving from place to place

oasis An area in a desert where plants grow because there is water. The plural of oasis is oases.

papyrus Material on which to write, made from a tall water plant or the plant itself

pesticide A chemical that is used to kill harmful insects

Pharaoh A ruler of ancient Egypt

pyramid A building of ancient Egypt used as a burial place, with four sides shaped like triangles that meet in a point at the top

reservoir A body of water that has been collected and stored for future use

restorer A person who works to bring back something to its original condition

sand dune A mound of sand formed by wind

spring A natural stream of water that flows from the earth

temple A building used for religious services

tomb A chamber or room for burying the dead

wadi A valley or river bed that remains dry except during the rainy season

worship To honor or respect a god

Index

1 2 3 4 5 6 7 8 9 0   Printed in the USA   5 4 3 2 1 0 9

Town Markets

A lantern maker.

A shoemaker.

A tailor.